Wither the Dead

A Biblical Treatise in Support of the Destruction of the Wicked in Final Judgment

Written by Request for Cross Winds Magazine
And Debated by Request With Dr. Gleason
Archer At the C.O.R. Arrow Head Springs
Conference, 1992

By

Rev. D. Earl Cripe, Ph.D.

Table of Contents

Wither The Dead
After Final Judgment

Whenever vital and controversial doctrines of the Christian faith are debated, emotions take a prominent role and views are frequently not formed on purely biblical lines. That is often not admitted as each polemicist feels certain that his interpretations are indeed one and the same with the words of the Bible. But such purity of mind and thought process is hard to find in any forum, and doubly so where feelings run high and traditional conviction takes precedence over sound biblical exegesis. In entering this arena, I hope not to enflame passions or wound sensitive souls. I have consented to this exercise in the belief that it is always advisable and never destructive to listen to a biblical point of view.

I feel it necessary to say that my mind is not immutably set on this issue. Like many men, I would suspect, I have moved around in my

1

thoughts and convictions and am not at the point where I can assure anyone that I am fully persuaded of a position and that I will move no more. The views that I shall advance here are, in my opinion, valid, biblical, and worthy of consideration. I do not offer them as dogma now (as I have not in the past) either in public or in private. I have no intention of allowing this exchange of articles, or any interactions that shall follow, to harden me into a position or to cast me in the role of defender in a matter where I lack such concreteness of resolve. Still, I will not consign myself to silence under threat of being branded unorthodox and I will not give up my right to independent and original thought in an area where the traditional teachings are not settled and irrefutable biblical doctrine, which on this subject they are not, in my view.

Three Basic Doctrines

Any meaningful discussion of the final determination of the unrighteous dead will necessarily ask three questions:

1. Is any part of natural born man — body, soul or spirit — immortal?

2. Does the Bible teach eternal, endless torment of the damned?

3. What does the Bible specifically and comprehensively say about hell?

Natural Man And Immortality

In antiquity, men were much more willing to engage this subject openly than fundamental theologians of today. The notion has frequently been put forward that there were few (if any) early Christian leaders who held any other doctrine than eternal torment. Such is simply not the case. The great Church historian Phillip Schaff notes, "In the West also at the time of Augustine there were, as he says, "multitudes who did not believe in eternal punishment."[1] There was an enthusiastic debate going on in the ante-Nicene, Nicene and post-Nicene Church on the question of the immortality of the soul of natural man. There was a great disparity of thinking and a wide

---

[1] Philip Schaff, *History of the Christian Church*, (WM. B. Eerdmans, Grand Rapids, Michigan, 1989), Vol. II, p. 612.

division between those who believed that the soul of natural man was immortal and those who believed that it was not. The Orthodox Fathers were divided on this doctrine, and therefore neither position can legitimately be called Orthodox in any settled sense. St. Augustine never made his own position very clear, in my view. He apparently believed in eternal torment, but an altered form of it. He had a place of peace and painlessness for unbaptized infants. Still they were damned. But even while holding that this tranquil place was part of eternal damnation and torment, he hedged on committing to an independently immortal soul in natural man, enigmatically seeing these as two different issues. He seemed at times to acknowledge that the Bible did not teach such a doctrine and to attribute its origin to Plato and the *Myth of Er*, though Plato's immortality envisioned only the soul, bereft of any physical body or status.[2] That St. Augustine was undecided and vacillating on the subject cannot

---

[2] Augustine, *City of God,* (Great Books; of the Western World, Encyclopedia Britannica Inc., Chicago, Ill., 1987), Vol. 18, p. 368.

be questioned. In chapter twenty-one of Book XII of *The City of God,* he says:

> "Man, on the other hand, whose nature was to be a mean between the angelic and the bestial, He created in such sort that if he remained in subjection to His Creator as his rightful Lord, and piously kept His Commandments, he should pass into the company of the angels and *obtain,* without intervention of death, a blessed and *endless immortality;* but if he offended the Lord his God by proud and disobedient use of his free will, he should become subject to death, and live as the beasts do."[3]

This seems to be a clear affirmation of Conditionalism in the Garden. Yet in Chapter 1 of Book XIII, entitled *Of the fall of the first man, through which mortality has been contracted,* he says:

---

3 *Ibid.* p. 357.

"But I see I must speak a little more carefully of the nature of death. For although *the human soul is truly affirmed to be immortal,* yet it also has a certain death of its own."[4]

Here St. Augustine appears to support intrinsic and inalienable immortality. Yet in Chapter 19 of Book XIII, entitled *Against the opinion of those who do not believe that the primitive men would have been immortal if they had not sinned,* he returns to Conditionalism by saying:

"Wherefore, if these philosophers will not dare (as I think they will not) to set human souls above the gods who are most blessed, and set are tied eternally to their bodies, why do they find that absurd which the Christian faith preaches, namely, that our first parents were so created that, if they had not sinned, they would not have been

[4] *Ibid.* p. 360.

dismissed from their bodies by any death, but *would have been endowed with immortality* as the reward of their obedience..."[5]

Arnobius believed in actual annihilation,[6] as did Hermas.[7] Justin Martyr believed natural man had "Natural immortality" and that this natural immortality would eventually destroy itself completely in the fires of judgment[8] Both Irenaeus and Justin denied any intrinsic immortality of the soul and made it dependent on God for the continuance in life, as well as for life itself.[9] Iranaeus, in *Against Heresies,* argued that man is free but still mortal. He must come to God through Jesus Christ — thus establishing obedience — in order to be immortal. Disobedience brings death. The Bible everywhere warns that the soul that sins shall die. Immortality is conditional and may be forfeited,

---

[5] *Ibid.* p. 370.
[6] Schaff, *History of the Christian Church,* Vol. II, p. 611.
[7] *Ibid.* p. 608
[8] *Ibid.* p. 610
[9] *Ibid*

so said Iranaeus[10] (though Irenaeus is said to have inconsistently held all available theories at one time or another). Contrary to prevalent thinking, this view has been popular with fundamental, evangelical theologians through the years. Some of the 19th century American theologians who held it are C.F. Hudson, W.R. Hunington, C.C. Baker, L.W. Bacon, and Horace Bushnell. Among the 20th century evangelical supporters of this view in one form or another are the late F.P. Bruce and John R. Stott. That the destruction of the wicked is held within the framework of orthodoxy is acknowledged by G. W. Grogan:

"Conditional Immortality is maintained by some of the sects... but also by some who, in other doctrines, stand within historic evangelicalism."[11]

---

[10] Iranaeus, *Against Heresies,* (The Ante-Nicene Fathers, T&T Clark/WM. B. Eerdmans, 1989) Vol. I, P. 522 (4.38.4; p. 551(5.23.1).

[11] G.W. Grogan, *The New International Dictionary of the Christian Church,* J. D. Douglas, Ph. D. General Editor (Zondervan Corporation, Grand, Rapids, Michigan, 1974), p. 250.

Philip Schaff warns that the effort to relegate the doctrine of Eternal Destruction from the world of Orthodox Christianity takes us beyond the realms of knowledge:

"After the general judgment we have nothing revealed but the boundless prospect of aeonian life and aeonian death. This is the ultimate boundary of knowledge.

"There was never in the Christian Church any difference of opinion concerning the righteous, who shall inherit eternal life and enjoy the blessed communion of God forever and ever. But the final fate of the impenitent who reject the offer of salvation admits of three answers to the reasoning mind..."[12]

Dr. R. Nicole sees orthodoxy, while not holding to non-eternal torment views in any

---

12 Schaff, *History of the Christian Church,* p. 606

majority number, as acknowledging the biblical case for complete destruction and therefore refusing to silence that view within its camp:

> "It [eternal torment] is inconsistent with God's love, it is urged, to allow any of his creatures to endure forever in torment. Furthermore, the continuance of evil would spell some area of permanent defeat for the divine sovereignty, a dark corner marring perpetually the glory of his universe. These considerations are not without weight, and a complete answer may not be possible in the present state of our knowledge."[13]

In spite of these widely fluctuating views, Philip Schaff, the great historian of the Church, has observed that "Everlasting Punishment of the wicked always was, and always will be the orthodox theory."[14] Perhaps so, but where

---

[13] R. Nicole, *Evangelical Dictionary of Theology,* ed. Walter Elwell, (Baker Book House, Grand Rapids, Michigan, 1984), p. 51.
[14] Schaff, *History of the Christian Church,* Vol. II, p. 606.

orthodox dogmas may not and cannot be challenged, theories can be.

The Destruction of the Wicked and the Councils of the Orthodox Church

An often-heard claim is that the Nicene and post-Nicene Church took up this matter in its councils and denounced as heresy Anhilationism, Conditional Immortality, or the destruction of the unredeemed, no matter how the doctrine is identified. Specifically it is charged that the Fifth Ecumenical Council of 553 A.D. (also known as the Second Constantinople Convention) denounced Conditional Immortality along with

Origenism[15] and Restorationism.[16] But this is a hopeful claim that is without foundation, so far as I am able to determine. Philip Schaff states that the only issues of substance that were

[15] *Origenism is* a complexity of numerous heresies, prominent among which are *Subordinationism* which sees Christ as an inferior, created being; *Preexistence and Pretemporal Fall of Human Souls* including the human soul of Christ; *Eternal Creation* which means that the creation was made immortal in the original creation and can never be destroyed; *Final Restoration* which means the extension of the work of redemption to inhabitants of planets, and the final restoration of every creature including fallen angels; *Origen's ascetic and docetistic Corporiety,* in which he not only believed that Christ was a phantom Who had no real physical existence but he doubted his own physical reality as well. This appears to have been due to his strong Gnostic leanings in which a perfect and pure being could not be physical. There were other matters of heresy as well including: ". . . his predilection for Plato . . . his leaning to idealism. . . his denial of a material resurrection. . . his neglect of grammatical and historical sense and his constant desire to find a hidden, mystic meaning. . ." in which he ". . .goes further in that direction than the Gnostics. . ." (Philip Schaff, *History of the Christian Church,* Vol. II, pp. 790-2). This caused Schaff to observe: "But his best disciples proved unfaithful to many of his most peculiar views, and adhered far more to the reigning faith of the Church. For—and in this too he is like Sehleiermacher—he can by no means be called orthodox, either in the Catholic or the Protestant sense. . . His leaning toward idealism. . . led him to many grand and fascinating errors." (*Ibid.,* p. 791)

[16] *Restorationism is* Origen's doctrine that the work of redemption extends to inhabitants of planets and stars and to all rational creatures and that all will be restored in the final analysis, not only of men but fallen angels.

discussed by the fifth council were the "Three Letters" and the issue of Monophysitism.[17] The Fifth Council, called by the Emperor Justinian without the concurrence of or agreement with the Pope, was attended by only 164 bishops in 451 A.D. (Chalcedon had been attended by more than 600[18]), and was never considered to be of much importance:

> "The fifth council was not recognized, however, by many Western bishops, even the vacillating Pope Vigilius gave in his assent to it, and it induced a temporary schism between Upper Italy and the Roman see. As to importance, it is far below the four previous councils. Its Acts, in Greek, with the exception of the fourteen anathemas, are lost."[19]

If there was any discussion of Origen and Origenism, it was in the context of the

---

[17] Schaff, *History of the Christian Church,* p. 351.
[18] *Ibid.*
[19] *Ibid.* pp. 351-2.

Monophysite doctrine.[20] The 11th anathema, which is disputed as an incongruous addition taken from the synod of 544 A.D., associates Origen with other heretics such as Arius, Eunomius, Madedonius, Apollinaris, Nestorius and Eutyches[21] (a group to which he no doubt belongs), but no mention or discussion of Conditional Immortality, nor any effort to associate it with Restorationism (with which it obviously has nothing in common) was taken up, as sometimes claimed.[22] I have made a review of other synods, councils and ecumenical councils of the ante-Nicene, Nicene and post-Nicene eras and find no instance where the subject was taken up and discussed, much less anathematized. It would appear that these views are brought forward by those who have confused lifelong beliefs with verifiable facts. Such is often the result of attempts to set forth as the sole orthodoxy, positions which are more emotional

---

[20] *Ibid.* pp. 770-71.
[21] *Ibid.* Footnote 1, p. 771
[22] *Ibid.* p. 771.

and traditional than substantive and biblical. (See Appendix A.)

Adam and Immortality

Was man made an immortal being at creation? The question would seem to answer itself. Certainly man was not given eternal life at creation. If he had been, then there could have been no death, for death is the antithesis of immortal life. Some men wish to extract the soul out of the equation. They concede that man's body was not immortal and that it will cease to exist after the final judgment. But, they argue, this is not true of the soul.

The question that we find necessary to ask is, where does this notion come from, and specifically, where is it taught in the Bible? It is not that Genesis doesn't comment on the subject. Indeed it does. But it does not say what those who hold for an immortal soul in natural man want it to say. After having warned them on pain of death not to disobey, God reflected on the plight of His recently fallen creation.

Gen 3:22 And the Lord God said, Behold, the man is become as one of us, to know good and evil: and now, lest he put forth his hand, and take also of the tree of life, and eat, and live for ever:

Gen 3:23 Therefore the Lord God sent him forth from the garden of Eden, to till the ground from whence he was taken.

Gen 3:24 So he drove out the man; and he placed at the east of the garden of Eden Cherubims, and a flaming sword which turned every way, to keep the way to the *tree of life*.

Several things are evident here. First, man sinned and would die. This meant that he would lose the life that God had fashioned with His hands and breathed into him. Secondly, there was life in the Garden that man did not have in the creation and that he did not receive while he was in the Garden. It is that life that is identified by the "Tree of Life." Man in the Garden, who had life from God in the creation, had the opportunity to add something to himself in terms of "life" if he had chosen to eat of the fruit of the Tree of Life instead of the fruit of the Tree of the Knowledge of Good and of Evil (or the Tree of *Knowing* Good and Evil, as it literally reads). And thirdly, God drove man out of the Garden so that he would not eat of the fruit of the Tree of Life because in his fallen state, it was no longer desirable for man to eat of this fruit. It is evident on its face that the life that this Tree had to offer was immortality: **"...and now, lest he put forth his hand, and take also to the tree of life, and eat, _and live forever_."** (Gen 3:22) It is also obvious that in chasing man out of the Garden and keeping him out, God was keeping man from becoming immortal. It was so that he would not live forever. This was an act of God's mercy. In that dramatic moment in the early history of the race, God resolved the issue. Man would not live forever in his sins. The prospect was too horrible. Not even God could contemplate it for long. His mighty voice trailed off as his aching heart began to envision the awfulness of the prospect: "...and now... lest he... live forever..."

The life that man could have gotten from the Tree of Life after the Fall was not everlasting life in the *happy and blissful sense.* The death of his spirit (in the sense that man no longer knew God personally and had fellowship with Him) had already taken place. God had already promised the Redeemer to bring life by faith and grace to the repentant. The die was already cast and no amount of eating of the Tree of Life was going to remit the curse at this point. What God was doing here was ensuring against the immortality of the damned. He would not allow that to happen.

I was raised in the orthodox, fundamental, evangelical Church, in which I have functioned as minister for twenty-seven years [and forty-seven years at the time of his passing. Ed.]. During the last half-century I have heard it said countless times that God made the soul of man eternal. He will either live eternal life or die eternal death. Life, it is often said, is not a question of existence, but of quality. You are alive if you are in the presence of God and said to be dead (though you are not actually) if you are separated from God.

As I have said I do not wish to get into an emotional discussion of that, but I do wish to join the issue on biblical grounds. I am unaware of any place in the Bible where that is clearly stated in so many words. I have read no Scripture that says that natural man is immortal in any sense whatsoever. Are you aware of any? Is there one that you can find by the most diligent search? I think not.

What Does the Bible Say?

The Bible nowhere teaches that the mortal soul of man is immortal or eternal. The Bible repeatedly says, from the second chapter of Genesis to the end of the Book, that the soul that sins shall _die_. But is it possible to deal specifically with the word "Immortality" and show from the Bible that man is not immortal and that he can only become immortal in Christ? Yes it is:

II Tim 1:8 ...according to the power of God;

II Tim 1:9 Who hath saved us, and called us with an holy calling, not according to our

works, but according to his owns purpose and grace, which was given us in Christ Jesus before the world began,

II Tim 1:10 But is now made manifest by the appearing of our Savior Jesus Christ, who hath abolished *death* and hath brought life and *immortality* to light through the gospel.

Here St. Paul says that death is the antithesis of immortality, and that immortality can only be had in Jesus Christ and the Gospel. Immortality can only be associated with life, not with death (the possibility of any correlation between death and immortality having been eliminated by God Himself in Genesis 3:22-24), therefore whatever you can call death, it is not and cannot be called *immortality*.

But does the Bible specifically say that natural man *does not* have immortality? Yes it does:

I Tim 6:14 ...until the appearing of our Lord Jesus Christ:

I Tim 6:15 Which in his times, he shall shew, who is the blessed and only Potentate, the King of kings and Lord of lords;

I Tim 6:16 *Who only hath immortality,* dwelling in the light which no man can approach unto; whom no man hath seen nor can see: to whom be honor and power everlasting, Amen.

Here St. Paul tells Timothy that God alone has immortality. It is said in such a context and teaching as to make it clear that Christ will give this immortality to those who are His at His coming, as indeed He has already given it to them in the present sense that they are resurrected with Him. But the point that is driven home with force is that God, not man, possesses immortality. This clearly denies that natural-born man has immortality in any sense. Romans 2:7 agrees fully with this when it refers to those who are seeking for immortality. Now if they are seeking for it, obviously they do not yet have it. While it may be true that this is talking about seeking something good, the point is nonetheless made that they do not have immortality. In I Corinthians 15:53-54, the Apostle says that this body is not immortal and that it must put on immortality in order to physically inherit the Kingdom of God. This is a further testimony against the notion that natural man has immortality.

The above mentioned citations are the only places in the Bible where immortality is named. In each case the point is made that natural man *does not* have immortality.

Some may wish to argue that man does not have an immortal body, but he does have an immortal spirit and soul. This is in no way satisfactory. Physical death had already been pronounced on Adam when he was driven from the Garden. Already the pronouncement had been made: "For dust thou art, and unto dust thou shalt return." It was not physical immortality (or certainly not that alone) that God was preventing Adam from obtaining. It was immortality in _any_ sense: body, soul or spirit, but specifically in this instance it seems that the matter of the soul and the spirit were being addressed. It is not sound biblical exegesis to argue that man could be denied physical immortality, but that God was powerless to deny him immortality of the spirit or soul because of the creation. These are Gnostic and Platonic notions that have no support from the Bible. It was Plato first who argued for the preexistence of human souls and that they had independent immortality and would go on existing for ever.

Conditional Immortality

Conditional Immortality

This is not an arcane or uncommon discussion among holy men. The ancients debated it and formulated a doctrine that was widely accepted, called the doctrine of Conditional Immortality. To many, (and perhaps most) scholars this has come to be viewed as an exclusively New Testament doctrine which says that man was not endowed with immortality naturally, and that it is only a gift of God through Jesus Christ. Those who do not believe in Christ ultimately come to a state of losing all physical and spiritual consciousness — in other words they cease to be (ostensibly through the destruction of the Judgment). While not wishing to argue with that concept, we must say that originally, Conditional Immortality encompassed the notion that man had an opportunity in the Garden to obtain immortality in an either-or kind of proposition. Man had one choice in this regard

— the Tree of Life, or the Tree of the Knowledge of Good and Evil with its promise of death. Man chose the Tree of the Knowledge of Good and Evil. Thus he failed to meet the condition by which his life might have become immortal. For free moral agency, this was a sad hour. But in the sovereignty of God, it was a great triumph. Had he chosen the Tree of Life first, man would have frozen himself in the eternal condition of finiteness and creatureliness. He would forever have remained a work of God's hands. He would never have known what it was like to be born of God, bone of His bone and flesh of His flesh. We have gained more in Christ than we lost in Adam. This is not to the credit of man's free choice, but to the glory of God's sovereignty and omniscience.

The choice of the Tree of the Knowledge of Good and of Evil over the Tree of Life was definitive. The condition was not met, so the option was taken away. When he fell, man lost his right to go on living, and God will take his life from him in an ultimate, complete and final sense in the day of judgment. The possibility of a fallen soul continuing to exist eternally was prevented by God when He drove man out of the Garden and placed Cherubim at the gate so that no one could eat of the fruit of the Tree of Life and live forever in his sins.

A Second Chance At Immortality

Through grace, the opportunity for man to obtain immortality has been returned. In the New Paradise of God stands the Tree of Life. But this is not offered to the natural, fallen man. It is only through Christ and through new birth into the new race. The old creation can die voluntarily with Christ on the cross, thus ridding himself of the old curse and putting an end to the child of Adam. This further shows that Adam's children do not possess immortality. If they did, their old life — body, soul and spirit — could not be eliminated from existence through the death of Christ. This underscores the New Testament principle of death, burial and resurrection, which means the end of the old man and the birth of the new, in every sense that resurrection and new life applies to the man. In admitting that man can

26

die and cease to exist in any sense as a child of Adam through the Cross of Christ, Orthodoxy is tacitly acknowledging that natural man does not possess inalienable immortality. It also shows how much Old Testament mentality — that of the reformation of the old creature — is masquerading around in the guise of Christianity.

The immortality of the natural soul is simply not found in the Bible. But this is exactly what those who believe in endless torment are saying. They teach that "life" is to be in the presence of God and that "death" is to be forever separated from God, in a condition of sin and torment. This puts an unnecessary burden on the mind as men try to comprehend the unity of the wrath and the love and mercy of God. And this, since it is unnecessary in this instance, is counterproductive to the mission of the Church. Some of the basis of its popularity lies in the fact that it can be considered to be inferred by certain subjects. Those who hold for the immortality of the natural soul are not evil men on that account, who are spurred on by inferior motives. Good men have struggled valiantly with this issue through the two thousand year history of the Church, driven by the best of intentions and desires. Still the doctrine cannot be supported by sound biblical exegesis, or so it seems to me.

Eternal Torment

Eternal Torment is the doctrine that the damned will suffer forever and ever, not being able to die because the mortal soul of man was made eternal by God. While numerous passages are interpreted to include the notion of Eternal Torment, there is relatively little Scripture to give it foundation and to serve as a point of departure. But those that do are certainly worthy of note. Chief among them is the teaching of Jesus that in hell the fire is not quenched and "their worm" (the little maggots) do not die. Along with this is the passage in Revelation 14:10-11 that speaks of the smoke ascending day and night for ever and ever as they are tormented in the presence of the Father and of the Holy Angels.

As for the Revelation passage, this is symbolism, and not only should not, but cannot be taken literally. There is no _night_ in heaven in eternity. If there were an _endless hell_, there would be no _day_ in it. The phrase "forever and ever," being literally "to the ages of the ages" does not in and of itself have the force of the _eternal_ or _endless_. It must receive that character from the context. In this case the context will not impart that meaning, for we do not believe or accept that the place where the wicked dead are to be tormented is in heaven itself, in _the presence of God_ and His heavenly hosts! Nor do we believe that it is likely or thinkable that God will _spend His eternal existence sitting there watching the damned suffer torment_. Yet this is what this passage _literally_ says. While God may do as He pleases, and vengeance is His to exact, applying Eternal Torment here is unnecessarily sinister and is not warranted by the _symbolic language_ of this text.

Conditional Immortality and Restorationism

An attempt is sometimes made to associate Conditional Immortality with Origenism and Restorationism. The basis for this inferred relationship is somewhat vague. It seems to be based on a notion that both doctrines have originated from humanism and Greek philosophy. But this is far from accurate in any sense. A brief summary of Restorationism should suffice to dispel the notion.

Philosophical Restorationism

The notion of the immortality of the soul first appears in Plato and the *Myth of Er*, as does the notion of Restorationism. This is linked to Plato's idea of the preexistence of human souls. For Plato, the soul was immortal long before it ever became embodied physically in this earth. Since it had no beginning in mortality, therefore it cannot end with mortality. It must endure forever. Plato recognized that men were under moral obligation, and he did believe that they would have to answer to God for their deeds. They will be punished by Rhadamanthus and Minos. Some bodies will not survive this punishment, but the soul is independently immortal. After the soul had been purged by fire (1,000 years would probably be sufficient) it would be restored to the presence of God in the immortal future.[23] Yet Plato did not think the destruction of the body is inevitable:

> "Ye who are sprung from a divine stock, consider of what works I am the parent and author. These (your bodies) are indestructible so long as I will it; although all that is composed can be destroyed."[24]

Still Plato prefers disembodied immortality of the soul.

---

[23] Schaff, *History of the Christian Church,* Vol. II, pp. 608-9.
[24] Augustine, *City of God, p.* 367.

"But this same Plato thinks that nothing better can happen to men than that they pass through life piously and justly, and, being separated from their bodies, be received into the bosom of the gods..."[25]

Gnosticism, taking platonic features for its foundation, also teaches immortality and Restoration. To Gnostics, salvation is a term that applies to the level of gnosis one achieves, and thus what level he will spend the future on. If true gnosis is achieved and the highest level is attained, man will be free from the inferiority and the scandal of physical being.

Religious or "Christian" Restorationism

Origen is the first so-called "Christian Gnostic" to come up with "Christian Universalism." Originally this applied to fallen angels and the devil himself, though he is said to have exempted the devil from final restoration in later years.[26] His views were rejected by the

---

[25] *Ibid.* p. 369.
[26] Schaff, *History of the Christian Church,* Vol. II, *p.* 611.

Orthodox Fathers and were anathematized by the local Synod of Constantinople in 543 A.D.:

> "Pusey contends (125-137) that Origen *was* condemned by the Fifth Ecumenical Council, but Hefele conclusively proves that the fifteen anathenatisms against Origen were Passed by a local Synod of Constantinople in 543 under Mennas."[27]

Scriptural Point of Departure

The Biblical basis for Restorationism (Universalism) seems to rest on one passage: "And I, if I be lifted up from the earth, will draw all men unto me" (John 12:32). There is not much to be learned from the Greek world *helko*, which means simply *to drag* or *to draw*. If there is a point to be made, it must hinge upon the context of thought. It is argued that since Jesus said earlier, in the 6th chapter, that no man could come to Him except the Father **"draw him"**, this is then teaching that man's will is not involved. It is

---

[27] *Ibid.* p. 612.

God's grace, mercy and sovereignty which, through the grace of Christ and the final end-workings of the Gospel, will bring all men to Himself.

Emotional and Rational Bases

But the greatest impetus for Restorationism is sentiment. Those who hold with this view refuse to see God as One who would let anyone suffer eternally. Since all, or most all, Restorationists believe in natural immortality, there is no alternative for them if man is not saved in the end, he will suffer eternally. The God of the Universalist, in His Sovereignty, Omniscience and Omnipotence, simply would not do that.

Restorationism and Orthodox Dogma

Orthodoxy rejects Restorationism as an orthodox theory because it fails to come to grips with the theme of the Gospel and the Great Commission. It ignores personal responsibility and decision, the need for repentance and conversion, the truth embodied in baptism — which is death, burial and resurrection resulting in new life into a new creation in the family of the

Second Adam. It makes the need for evangelism superfluous, removes the warning of condemnation and actually eliminates the basis for the judgment, which Hebrews 6:2 identifies as a _foundation doctrine_ of the orthodox Christian faith (even Plato did not do that). The meager biblical support for the idea simply cannot be allowed to stand in the face of such overwhelming biblical opposition and contradiction. We do not deny the words of Jesus, but feel that this "drawing" cannot be an irresistible, sovereign force as in election, but a wooing that can be ignored, denied or rejected. The anathema pronounced on Restorationism by orthodoxy is fully justified in the light of the Scripture.

Restorationism and Eternal Torment

Wherever the lines fall, there is one set of observations that cannot be denied. Restorationism and Eternal Torment have natural immortality in common. Eternal Torment and Conditional Immortality have the Fall, the Incarnation, the Cross, the Resurrection and the Gospel mandate in common. But Restorationism and Conditional Immortality have nothing at all in common.

Restorationism's Claim to Orthodoxy Denied

Restorationists argue that all three theories have the redemption of the Cross and the power of the resurrection in common. All men needed saving, and Christ died for all men. Vicarious atonement for the sins of the whole world was put into force by a sovereign act that did not depend on man's recognition or acceptance. Orthodoxy answers that Christ is the propitiation, *not for our sins only,* but *also for the sins of the whole world* (I John 2:2), thus making a distinction between those who accept the gift and those who do not. God will have all men to be saved, but not all men will be saved. The fact that Christ died for all does not impose salvation upon all. He that *believes* is not condemned, but he that *believes not* **is** condemned already because he has not believed on the name of the only begotten Son of God.

Restorationism and Foreordination

The doctrine of Restorationism denies the doctrine of Preterition. It says that no one is passed over by God or predestined to be lost. This runs afoul of the Scriptures which tell us that Judas fell so that he might go to his own place (Acts 1:25), of those who were of old ordained to condemnation (Jude 4) and of those who were made to be taken and destroyed and who shall utterly perish in their own corruption (II Pet 2:12).

A Syncretic Claim

Restorationism and Conditional Immortality are not blown by the same theological winds as are Torment and Restoration. It is hard to see a commonality between Eternal Destruction and Restorationism *if* natural man is intrinsically immortal, and *if* God, in His goodness, cannot and will not allow any man to be sentenced and destroyed. The effort to associate Restorationism with Conditional Immortality (in any sense that has significance or meaning) must be discounted as a tactic to establish a bias against Conditional Immortality by those who believe in Eternal Torment, but who cannot advance either their apologetic or

37

polemical views on the subject by sound biblical exegesis.

About Hell

An essential consideration in a dialogue of this nature is what exactly the Bible says about hell. A comprehensive analysis of this subject would take a book of considerable length, perhaps two. But for this purpose, we will take a brief look.

Gehenna

Gehenna is the Valley of Hinnom, a gorge outside Jerusalem where the refuse of the city was dumped and where the fires were burning continually. Jesus used this term metaphorically to symbolize the judgment of God against all that was impure and defiling to the life and the Kingdom of God. While many men have wanted to see this as the place of torment, clearly the Valley of Hinnom is not the place of the departed damned where they are in torment. Jesus said that it is better to go through life with one eye than to have two eyes and to "be cast into that place where the fire is not quenched and their worm dieth not." This is a difficult passage for those who do not see an eternal torment in a place of burning fire if they attempt to deal with the words of Jesus in the context of _hell_. The fact is, however, that Jesus did not use the word _Hades_ when he gave these teachings. What he said was **"to be cast into Gehenna."**

Jesus knew the word _Hades_. He used it when he talked about the rich man who lifted up his eyes being in torment and talked to Abraham about the torment of the flames. He also used the word _Hades_ when he warned Chorazin and Bethsaida of impending judgment, in St. Luke 10:13-15. The question in Mark 9:43 is not one of how to explain away the unquenchable fire and the maggots that never die because they are feeding eternally on the unconsumed flesh. It is, rather, one of subject and context. What was Jesus talking about? The fact is that he was not talking about _Hades_, His audience was Jewish and every one of them knew about the _Valley of Hinnom_. They knew exactly what Jesus was talking about. It was about the fires of judgment and purification. They may not have discerned the spiritual depth of those teachings, but they understood the metaphor. Remember that Jesus did not say that having one eye is better than having two eyes and being cast into _hell_. He said it is better to go through life with one eye than having two eyes and being cast into _Hinnom_, or _Gehenna_. Jesus' teaching was _not about hell_, it was about the principle of making choices and suffering the consequences. He was teaching men that it is better to deny oneself the indulgences of the flesh in order to have the blessing of God and the peace that comes with righteousness than to have everything you want, but to suffer the judgment that comes along with it. This is a judgment that does not go away overnight like a headache. It is one that stays with a man, eats into his soul, dogs his steps and hounds him to the very grave. The fires of this burning never go out because they are constantly fueled by the evil works that brought on the judgment. It is the devil's lie that we can harden our conscience and do the thing today, and that tomorrow the conscience will return and we can go on as if nothing had happened. You really cannot have it both ways. Sin brings death. There is no getting around it and there is no getting back the life, the joy and the reward that we threw away by wrong choices. Gehenna answers to that body of knowledge and thought that gives rise to the sayings, "hell is right here on this earth," and "men make their own hell in this life." There is truth to that persuasion, so long as it is not made the whole meaning of hell. It becomes a heresy when it attempts to deny the reality of Hades and the consequences for sin in the future judgment.

Is a Literal Interpretation of This Passage Possible?

Perhaps you do not agree with my interpretation. That is quite alright of course, but let me ask you this question: do you have only one eye and one hand, the other eye having been plucked out so that you would never again look at that woman with lust, and the other hand having been cut off when you used it to accomplish some unsanctified act? Or will you go out straight away after having read this, and cut that hand off and pluck that eye out? Apparently, then, you do not believe that it is to be taken literally either. And if it is, do you know anyone who is going to escape the fires of endless torment? How many one-eyed, one-handed Christians have you seen in your lifetime who were in that state as a consequence of taking literally this passage? And if this teaching is to be taken literally, how will this prevent the man from sinning? What is to keep him from using the remaining eye to look with lust? It thus appears that the man will have to blind himself, and then of course we still have not dealt with the matter of the thoughts and imaginations of the mind. These are inevitably the kinds of blind alleys we wind up in when we attempt to take the letter instead of the spirit of truth in a text that was obviously not intended to be taken literally. Whatever Jesus meant in this passage which refers to Gehenna, it _cannot be used_ to build a _strong biblical or theological case_ for Eternal Torment.

Gehenna and the Lake of Fire

Many of those who believe in eternal torment consider Gehenna to be the Lake of Fire and Hades, the present place of the wicked dead, to be a temporary place. That is an interesting theory, but it can be no more than that, for Jesus did not say that Gehenna was the Lake of Fire, and the literal Gehenna was certainly not. I do not object to symbols and allegories in the Bible, of course. But it seems to me that there would have to be something more definitive to establish the point before it could take on the stature of settled dogma.

Sheol

Sheol is a Hebrew word meaning _the grave_ but also projects beyond that to the place of torment for the departed damned, where they will be held until the day of Judgment. Acts 2:24-32 makes it one and the same with Hades.

Hades

Hades really means the _unseen place_, or the place where the unrighteous dead go after death and are not seen. It is the Greek word for _hell_, meaning the literal place of torment for the departed damned, where they are held until the day of Judgment, at which time Hades gives them up (Rev 20:13). Is hell real? Is there such a place where the unrighteous dead are in torment? Jesus said there was, in St. Luke 17:23. The liberal argument that this was just a parable cannot be taken seriously. Jesus did not say it was a parable. He used the names of actual people, which He never did in parables, and certainly Abraham is not a fictional character. There is nothing metaphorical about _Hades_, as there is with _Gehenna_. The question is not one of whether or not there is a real, burning hell. The question is, what (if anything) does the Bible tell us about the future of this place, as well as those that are in it?

Hell Gives Up The Wicked Dead

The Bible teaches, in Revelation 20:13-17, that hell will be emptied of its contents, who will then stand before God in judgment. Once having given up their dead, death and hell are cast into the Lake of Fire, evidently for the purpose of destruction. The unrighteous dead are not put back into hell, but are cast into the Lake of Fire along with death, hell, the dragon, the beast and the false prophet. It is not necessary to understand all of the symbolism and just exactly what all is being portrayed to see that a major change — with respect to hell and the grave where the dead are, and the place of the unrighteous dead — takes place at and after the final Judgment. I Corinthians 15:26 says that the second coming of Christ and the events that comprise the final Judgment will _destroy death_. Evidently this Revelation passage means to tell us that hell is destroyed too, along with the devil, every evil angel, unrighteous men and every evil work (the context of Revelation 20:13-17 is works).

Judgment a Part of Love, Mercy and Redemption

When the redemptive processes of God in Christ Jesus have completed their outworking in this world (culminating at the Resurrection and the Judgment) every evil being and every evil thing will have been eliminated from existence forever. There will never, throughout all the ages of eternity, be any remembrance of evil again forever. There will be no more sin, death, sickness, pain, crying, loneliness or any other inferior thing. All of those former things have passed away. All that God has done for man, from before the world was created, was for this purpose. God saw the wicked before He ever created them. He has given them their opportunity to live on this earth, to have being and to know life, such as it has been. But they have forfeited their right to go on living. Time-and-history is real and God reacts to it (in infralapsarianism), but in His supralapsarian plan for the ages, He has control over all. God is not a fiend whose vengeance is insatiable. He is not going to be a prison keeper who presides eternally over the torture of the damned. He is not going to be haunted forever by the terrified, agonized screams of those who will go on being tortured forever with no hope of relief. Nor did God set in motion a force, when he made man, that he cannot control or destroy. God is God, not a Dr. Frankenstein who is the helpless victim of his own creative invention and mistake. When God made man, He promised him that He would take from him the life that was given him, in the day that man would sin (God offered man the chance to obtain immortality, but man did not take it, and because of the Fall it was taken away). For those who do not find redemption in Christ, that is exactly what He will do.

Annihilation

It is often supposed that the doctrine of Annihilation is one and the same with Conditional Immortality, and that each of these is identical with the doctrine of the Eternal Destruction of the Wicked. This is not the case, and the differences are of more than a little importance, at least to me. Consider this rephrasing of Warfield:

"The word is from the Latin *nihil,* "nothing," and expresses the position of those who hold that some, if not all, human souls will cease to exist after death. As observed by Warfield, this point of view may take three main forms: (1) that all human beings inevitably cease to exist altogether at death (materialist); (V that, while human beings are naturally mortal, God imparts to the redeemed the gift of immortality and allows the rest of humanity to sink into nothingness (conditional immortality); (3) that man, being created immortal, fulfills his destiny in salvation, while the reprobates fall into nonexistence either through a direct act of God or through the corrosive effects of evil (Annihilationism proper). The distinction between Conditionalism and Annihilationism, as indicated above, is frequently not observed..."[28]

Annihilationism argues that man was created immortal and that he loses this immortality if he does not go on to fulfill his mortal destiny, which is to find salvation. With this doctrine I do not agree. Conditional Immortality holds that man never had immortality, having forfeited the opportunity in the Garden, and that he can only find it through the life and immortality that Christ has brought to light through the Gospel. The condition which is then put upon finding immortality is accepting Christ and His Gospel. In this view, one cannot have immortality without having salvation, and one cannot have salvation without having immortality.

The Eternal Destruction of the Wicked Dead

Up to this point, Conditional Immortality is not unlike the view advanced by this paper. The

---

[28] Nicole, *Evangelical Dictionary of Theology,* ed. Walter Elwell, p. 50.

critical question is, where does Conditional Immortality go now? The answer is hard to pin down, but the issues, insofar as I am concerned, are not. If, as Nicole cites Warfield, man who does not have salvation and has therefore not found immortality, "sinks into nothingness;" if this is Justin's doctrine of "natural immortality eventually destroying itself," then I cannot go along. If on the other hand these vague statements by critics are designed to be imprecise and to create a nebulous and ambiguous future for the unsaved; if Conditional Immortality in fact believes that the wicked are tried, condemned and destroyed with an eternal destruction, I have no problem with that as to the findings of this paper.

Pat Phrases

One of the problems with pat phrases is that they often become self-contained doctrines that are limited to the parameters of the phrase as any given person sees it. Thus they isolate the subject identified by the phrase from biblical exegesis and real discussion. What is then important is not what the Bible says, but what this phrase has come to mean to religious men. That is why I prefer the concept of the "eternal destruction of the wicked" to the phrases *Annihilationism* or *Conditional Immortality*. The thought of the everlasting destruction of the wicked is much easier to examine from a biblical perspective.

The Nature and Character of Judgment

In Hebrews 6:2 we are told that one of the fundamental doctrines of the faith is that of the eternal judgment. St. Jude says that the fallen angels are being reserved for the judgment of that great day. Sodom and Gomorrha and the cities of the plain, which defied God and made evil their preoccupation, are an example of that great judgment. They suffered **"...the vengeance of eternal fire."** Sodom and Gomorrha were *eternally destroyed* by *the fires* of *God's judgment*. They are forever gone from existence and they shall never rise from the ashes. In fact, not even the ashes can be found. But this eternal judgment of fire does not mean that they are in a continual state of burning. If you go over to the ancient sites and look around, you will feel no heat from glowing embers and see no smoke clouding the sky from the destruction of Sodom and Gomorrha. To be forever destroyed by the fires of God's judgment does not mean, in this instance at least, to *be forever in the process of being destroyed.* As to destruction, there is a contradiction in that very concept. If something is *forever in the process of being destroyed,* then it will never be *destroyed completely.* But clearly this is not what happened to Sodom and Gomorrha. They *were destroyed completely* from the face of the earth, and that Judgment *will* abide *forever* upon them. With this example before the hearer, St. Jude goes on to say of the wicked: **"The Lord cometh with ten thousands of his saints, *to execute judgment* upon all, and to convince all that are ungodly among them of all their ungodly deeds which they have ungodly committed, and of all their hard speeches which ungodly sinners have spoken against him"** (Jude 1:14-15). In II Thessalonians

1:8-9, St. Paul says a similar thing when he tells of the time when the Lord will come with His mighty angels, **"...In flaming fire taking vengeance on them that know not God, and obey not the gospel of our Lord Jesus Christ: who shall be punished with <u>everlasting destruction</u> from <u>the presence of the Lord and from the presence of His power</u>, when *He* shall come to be glorified in his saints, and to be admired in all them that Believe (because our testimony among you was believed) in <u>that day</u>."** Not only does this show us plainly that Revelation cannot be speaking of eternal torment of the wicked after judgment (the torment there is *in the presence* of the holy angels and *the presence* of the Lamb), but the final judgment of God will destroy them forever and that destruction will *remove them from His presence.*

The Epistemological Problem Of Eternal Torment

The Omnipresent God

Some men would answer this matter by saying that there is a place of outer darkness, were God *is not* nor *ever has been* and will *never go*. This doctrine, which smacks of Karl Barth's *Dualism,*[29] denies the omnipresence of God. It

---

[29] To Barth, there was an evil nonexistent existence, a non-created chaos, that preexisted with God (Barth, *Church Dogmatics,* Vol. III/1, p.112). It could not have been created by God, because it was evil. The non-created non-reality exists by virtue of its being separated from God *(Grundrize, p.* 65). It had meaning only in that it had *no* meaning, since God left it behind Him without giving it existence *(C.D., Vol. II, p.84).* It had essence in that God did not think about it; He put it behind His back and passed it by *(CD.* m/l, o. 112). God could not have made the decision to not think about it unless it were there (*Ibid*). The Chaos—though rejected—*was active as a shadow which also lay on the world which God willed and created.* God *passed it by,* thus making it a part of the *eternal past,* which was never *present* or *now.* Yet the *shadow is* still real and becomes *active and actual* when man *rejects, ignores or forgets true choices.* Foolish man can look back and, in so doing, become a part of the *past,* swallowed up in the *dark chaos,* which is then a very real danger again, not because it *has invaded the present,* which *it has not* and *cannot,* but because man has lapsed into the *uncreated, never-present, eternally rejected past* (*Ibid.* p. 119).

says that there is a place, whether or not it exists or was created, where God is not and cannot go. It is a place that God has put behind His back, or at least will after final Judgment. Throughout all eternity God will not know that it is there. But it is there! And people, perhaps reduced to the status of not being people but still existing, are there. This flies in the face of the Scriptures on two accounts.

The Scriptural Testimony of God in Hell

In Psalm 139:6-12, King David the Prophet said: **"Such knowledge is too wonderful for me; it is high, I cannot attain unto it. Whither shall I go from thy spirit: or whither shall I flee from thy presence: If I ascend up into heaven, thou are there: if I make my bed in *hell,* behold, thou are there. If I take the wings of the morning, and dwell in the uttermost parts of the sea; Even there shall thy hand lead me, and thy right hand shall hold me. If I say, Surely the darkness shall cover me; even the night shall be light about me. Yea, the darkness hideth not from thee; but the night**

shineth as the day: the darkness and the light are both alike to thee." Verse 15 probably indicates that this is a Messianic Psalm about Christ in the three days of His death and descension into hell. In any case it shows dearly that God is in hell in the omnipresent sense and that the darkness hides no one from God. This is the darkness of _hell,_ not just _any_ darkness. It is sometimes answered that the Old Testament Sheol means, and only means, the grave. The problem with that is that St. Peter quoted another Messianic Psalm, 16:8-10, in Acts 2:25-28, where he fully establishes that Sheol is Hades, the place of the wicked dead.

The Soteriological Problem

Where did Christ go and what did He suffer in his substitutionary death for us? The Orthodox doctrine of Vicarious Suffering is that Jesus Christ, in order to make expiation for sins, was made sin for us. He took our place in judgment, was condemned in the court of God and went into hell, the place of the damned for us, because that was what we deserved and that was the condemnation we were under.

Isa 53:8 He was taken from prison and from judgment: and who shall declare his generation? for he was cut off out of the land of the living: <u>for the transgression of my people was he stricken</u>.

Isa 53:9 **<u>And he made his grave with the wicked</u>, and with the rich in his death; because he hath done no violence, neither was any deceit found in his mouth.**

Isa 53:10 Yet it pleased the Lord to bruise him; he hath put him to grief: <u>when thou shalt make his soul an offering for sin</u>, he shall see his seed, he shall prolong his days, and the pleasure of the Lord shall prosper in his hand.

Isa 53:11 He shall see of the <u>travail of his soul</u>, and shall be satisfied: by his knowledge shall my righteous servant justify many; for he shall <u>bear their iniquities</u>.

II Cor 5:21 For He hath <u>made him to be sin for us</u>, that we might be made the righteousness of God in him.

Acts 2:25 For David speaketh concerning him, I foresaw the Lord always before my face, for he is on my right hand, that I should not be moved:

Acts 2:26 Therefore did my heart rejoice, and my tongue was glad; moreover also my flesh shall rest in hope:

Acts 2:27 Because thou wilt not leave my soul in hell, neither wilt thou suffer thine Holy One to see corruption.

Acts 2:28 Thou hast made known to me the ways of life; thou shalt make me full of joy with thy countenance.

Acts 2:29 Men and brethren, let me freely speak unto you of the patriarch David, that he is both dead and buried, and his sepulchre is with us unto this day.

Acts 2:30 Therefore being a prophet, and knowing that God had sworn with and oath to him, that of the fruit of his loins, according to the flesh, he would raise up Christ to sit on his throne;

Acts 2:31 He seeing this before spake of the resurrection of Christ, that his soul was not left in hell, neither did his flesh see corruption.

Acts 2:32 This Jesus hath God raised up, whereof we are all witnesses.

Rom 4:22 And therefore it was imputed unto him [Abraham] for righteousness.

Rom 4:23 Now it was not written for his sake alone, that it was imputed to him;

Rom 4:24 But for us also, to whom it shall be imputed, if we believe on him that raised up Jesus our Lord from the dead;

Rom 4:25 Who was <u>delivered for our offenses</u> and raised for our justification.

Heb 5:7 Who in the days of his flesh, when he had offered up prayers and supplications with <u>strong crying and tears unto him that was able to save him from death, and was heard in that he feared</u>,

Heb 5:8 Though he were a Son, yet learned he obedience through the things that he suffered;

Heb 5:9 And being made perfect, he became the author of eternal salvation unto all them that obey him.

Heb 9:24 For Christ is not entered into the holy places made with hands, which are figures of the true; but into heaven itself, now to appear in the presence of God for us:

Heb 9:25 Nor yet that he should offer himself often, as the high priest entereth into the holy place every year with the blood of others;

Heb 9:26 For then must he often have suffered since the foundation of the world: but now once in the end of the world hath he appeared *to* put away sin by the sacrifice of himself.

Heb 9:27 And as it is appointed unto men once to die, but after this the judgment:

Heb 9:28 So Christ was once offered to bear the sins of many; and unto them that look for him shall he appear the second time without sin unto salvation.

I Pet 2:24 Who his own self bare our sins in his own body on the tree, that we, being

dead to sins, should live unto righteousness: by whose stripes ye were healed.

Acts 2:23 Him being delivered by the determinate counsel and foreknowledge of God, ye have taken, and by wicked hands have crucified and slain:

Acts 2:24 Whom God hath raised up, <u>having loosed the pains of death: because it was not possible that he should be holden of it</u>.

Several things would seem to be evident here. If the penalty for sin is eternal torment, then Christ did not suffer our judgment, because He is not in eternal torment and will not be in it forever. If there is a place of eternal torment which is the real and eternal meaning of hell, where God has never gone and never will go and cannot go, then Christ did not go into hell for our sins, which means that the statements by the Prophet David and St. Peter are false and misleading. If the penalty for sin is eternal torment in this dualistic monstrosity where the Omnipresent God cannot go, and if Christ went into another hell which is not the eternal penalty for sin, then how is He our substitute, how has He suffered our judgment, how has He made expiation for our sins, how have the legal demands of the Atonement been satisfied and what makes us think that we are free from condemnation?

Death Is the Penalty for Sins

If there is one thing that the Bible declares from Genesis to Revelation, it is that death is the penalty for sins. This is put in contrast to eternal life. Once death takes place, the body corrupts, for it is mortal and wracked by sin. Christ did indeed take our place in judgment and suffer our penalty. That penalty was death, Hades, judgment and execution. Once this was done, the sentence was carried out and propitiation had been affected. The wrath was appeased and peace was made. Expiation (the means by which reparation was made) was carried out, and atonement (the legal requirement for reparation) was met. It was never intended that the body, soul and spirit of Christ should go into eternal torment, because that was never the biblically prescribed punishment for sin. And so, once having made the substitutionary sacrifice and having effected the atonement, the body of Christ rose from the grave, being quickened by the Spirit (I Pet 3:18). Why? Because not being sinful or mortal (though real, human and in the likeness of sinful flesh), it could not corrupt. Christ's body was not fashioned from the dust of the ground. He was conceived by the Holy Ghost. Corruption was not a punishment for sin, but a natural consequence of the mortal body dying. Man would return to the dust from whence he came when the life that God breathed into him was taken from him. But Christ, as Isaiah pointed out, was assured by the Father from the beginning that sacrificial death for the sins of the world would not result in his destruction and demise. He would not leave Him in hell and He would not let His body corrupt. When the Father sent the Son to be the Savior of the world (I John 4:14), the Son accepted the assignment (Phil 2:6-8) upon the assurance that death, not corruption and endless suffering, was the expiation for sin. He had our sins upon him, but He knew no sin. He was made sin for us, but He had no sins of His own. Those who are Christ's will be resurrected, just as He was, in the day of Christ's return. **"Christ the first fruits, then they that are Christ's at His coming"** (I Cor 15:23) But it will not be the old creation, born to Adam (I Cor 15:20-26). It will be the body that is of the Second Adam, not "of the earth earthy," but the "Lord from heaven." The old man is forever dead, having died with Christ on the Cross (Rom 6:3-11). It is the New Man, born again in immortality to the Second Adam and the New Creation (II Cor 5:16-17, I Pet 3:18, I Cor 15:42-54). This birth is of incorruptible seed which lives and abides forever, according to the Apostle in I Peter 1:23.

If eternal torment was the punishment for sin, then none of this would have happened. Christ, once having died for sin, would either have lain in the grave awaiting the day of judgment and being cast into eternal torment _or_ He would have been cast into eternal torment at His death (temporal suffering in Hades would not be sufficient, as it would not meet the requirement of taking our place in judgment). This would be inevitable if natural man were immortal. It would have been inevitable if God had let Adam eat of the fruit of the Tree of Life. In that consequence, no expiation or atonement could have been made, for the Righteous God could not suffer forever in torment. But God did not let Adam eat of the Tree of Life. This was a key time-and-history action by God to leave open the avenue for the redemption of man.

Eternal Destruction

Thus we see orthodox Soteriology demands that the punishment for the wicked dead is a death that is eternal, not a tortured form of eternal existence because of an imagined state of natural immortality that simple does not exist in the pages of the Bible.

The Etymological Problem

Eternal, Forever, Forever More, Everlasting, Etc.

One of the main arguments for eternal torment is founded upon the belief that the terms _eternal_, _everlasting_, _forever_, _forever more_, and so on, mean, and can only mean something that endures throughout all eternity. I have two comments to make about this.

An Example of What is Meant by the Vengeance of Eternal Fire

1. Many, indeed the vast majority of times, those terms do mean to reflect eternity. But that does not tell the whole story. What is it that lasts throughout the endlessness of eternity? Is it the fact that the wicked are no more, having been executed? (Rom 6:3-11) Or is it the fact that they are eternally in the process of dying? In both cases we have a condition that exists forever.

The cities of Sodom and Gomorra suffered the vengeance of eternal fire, but they are not still burning. If you go over there and look, you will see no smoke and feel no glowing embers. The point is that the fires of God's judgment destroyed them, and they shall remain destroyed forever, never to arise from the ashes. When something exists throughout all eternity, it does not necessarily mean that it is in an ongoing process. St. Peter says that in the day of the Lord, this old creation — this heavens and earth that were created in six days in Genesis 1 and 2 — being on fire, will melt with fervent heat, will be burned up and dissolved and will be destroyed from existence, to be replaced by a New Heavens and a New Earth, according to the New Testament principle of death, burial, regeneration and new life as opposed to the reformation of the Genesis flood. The destruction of the present heavens and earth will remain as a fact for all eternity. But that does not mean that the destruction of the present heavens and earth will be going on all of that time. It will be an eternal judgment of fire that will result in an everlasting destruction. But it will not be an eternal destroying. So it is with the wicked dead. Everlasting destruction does not mean to be everlastingly at the process of destroying. Everlasting death does not mean to be everlastingly in the process of dying. The wages of sin is _death,_ not _a tortured form of eternal life,_ which is a pitiful concept of the loving judgment of the Great God (loving, because final judgment is designed to remove from existence death with all of its consequences and the rot of evil forever). It is partly due to biblical misunderstanding, partly owing to the inherent fear and foreboding in man, and somewhat owing a mystical concoction that is part Gnostic, part Platonic and part Roman myth. An eternal, living condition of the unrighteous dead after final judgment, however it is defined, is nowhere taught in the Bible.

Eternal life is active forever because, unlike death, it is an ongoing process. Christ is _alive forever more! So_ are we who believe. The point to be observed here is not the word _forever,_ but the difference between _life_ and _death._

When Continually or Perpetually Does Not Mean Throughout All Eternity

2. And then, *forever, eternal* and *everlasting* do not always mean something that lasts throughout the endless ages of eternity. All of these words are the same: *eons,* or *to the eons of the eons (the ages of the ages).* This word/s, which means *continually,* or *to perpetuity,* has a time limitation built into it. The Bible speaks about before the *eons* began (II Tim 1:9, Tit 1:2) and of the end of the *eons.* (I Cor 10:11, Heb 9:26) Of course the Bible uses the term *eons* to speak of eternity as well in St. Mark 8:36, Ephesians 1:21 and 3:21. Because of the difficulty we have in speaking of timeless, ageless eternity, the term to the *ages of the ages* is most often used to represent this concept (though the word *ages* is not used that way in the majority of cases). But the phrase itself does not demand that meaning. Its limits and parameters must be understood from the context.

In Ecclesiastes 1:4, Solomon said, **"One generation passeth away, and another**

generation cometh: but the earth abideth _**forever.**_**"** I doubt that there is anyone reading this who has not had encounters with Jehovah's Witnesses who try to use this verse to convince us that the Bible says this earth will never be destroyed. We try to convince them otherwise. Solomon was not talking about how long the earth would be here. He was talking about the temporality of man and the frustration and limitations of mortality. A man cannot get anywhere in the strictly mortal system. Neither can the earth around us. It is a testimony of futility. The sun rises and begins setting, only to rise again, the wind goes around in circles, the rivers carrying on their weary cycle of running to the sea, only to be evaporated back up into the atmosphere, drift back over the mountains, fall as rain and run to the sea again. Yet the sea never rises. It is an endless process. This accomplishes nothing. It is vanity in action. There is nothing new in this world. Everything is going around in endless, futile cycles and passing on. Man comes and goes, but the earth goes on continually. In this case, *forever* does not mean *throughout all eternity*.

In Jeremiah 7:7, God tells the wayward Israelites that if they will amend their ways, they may dwell in the land which He gave to their fathers forever and ever. This does not appear to be a case where the New Testament and the New, Eternal Kingdom is in view. It has to do with the corrupted worship of the nation and God's warning to them about it. In saying that He had given this land to them *forever and ever*, God was not denying the future destruction of this heavens and earth. He did not mean by this, that this land would belong to the nation of Israel *throughout the endless ages of eternity*. The term has to be understood in the light of the context and what we know of God's plan for the ages. It simply means "continually," as long as the covenant is in force. There are *many* similar usages in the Old Testament.

In Revelation 14:10-11, we are told that those who worship the beast and receive his mark shall be tormented day and night in the presence of the Holy Angles and of the Lamb, and the smoke of their torment shall descend up *day and night for ever and ever.* Obviously this does not mean throughout all eternity, unless you think that the place where the wicked are going to be eternally punished is in the presence of Christ and His people, and that the throne room of God is going to be smogged over throughout all eternity with the smoke of the burning damned. In this case the phrase *to the ages of the ages* or *continually* means to tell us that whatever is going on here (and whenever it is going on), it is a continual activity so long as this situation and condition lasts.

The Analogy of the Scripture

The Analogy of the Scripture is a phrase which means *comparing Scripture with Scripture.* In the 18th century, Bishop Newton said: "Make the Word of God as much as possible it's own interpreter. You will best understand the Word of God by comparing it with itself, 'comparing spiritual things with spiritual' (I Cor 2:13)." In the 16th century, Bishop Lowth said: "Scripture doth best interpret itself." These quotes, along with multitudes of others that we could cite, form the Historic Orthodox precept of Bible teaching and preaching. No doctrine, principle or supposed biblical idea that is founded upon a single text is part of the analogy of faith. That is why the Orthodox Fathers were against topical teaching. Theology is the whole meaning of the Scriptures — that is, it is the sense and the theme of the Bible as modeled, limited and explained by Scripture itself. *It is impossible for the theology of the Bible to be one thing, and the meaning of a scriptural passage to be another.* What is true of passages is true of words as well. There is an orthodox caution against trying to build theology out of words alone. Certainly the Bible is comprised of words, and certainly words have meaning. But they must be disciplined by the context if they are to convey truth to us. If a text without a context is a pretext, a word without a context is even more so. With *eons* or *to the eons of the eons*, it is the words taken in context that will give us the meaning, and not the meaning of the words alone.

The Deontological Problem

All orthodox theologians agree fully that sentiments, emotions, feelings and intellectual perceptions are not the stuff that sound doctrine is made of. We do not formulate doctrine on sentiment, but on the Scripture. God is right and His acts are right, no matter how we feel about it. Yet feelings are a part of man and are not wrong or misleading so long as they are kept in perspective. There is nothing wrong with feeling joy, thankfulness and relief at hearing the message of Justification. The power and the truth is not in the feelings, they are in the Bible and the message of truth. But such emotions are indeed proper as the result of hearing, comprehending and truly accepting the message. Sentimental reactions to the teachings of the Bible are inevitable. Negative feelings of resentment and revulsion also effect man's willingness and ability to make choices. If such feelings are brought on by the unequivocal and unavoidable truth, there is nothing that we can (or would want to) do about it.

Man's Perception of God

The matter of how He is perceived is not a thing of indifference to God. The Bible is replete with statements and arguments to project and support the love, kindness, gentleness, patience, long-suffering and pity of God. In Psalm 26:3, David says of the Lord: **"Thy lovingkindness is before mine eyes."** In Psalm 48:9-10: **"We have thought of thy lovingkindness, O God, in the midst of thy temple. According to thy name, O God, so is thy praise unto the ends of the earth: thy right hand is full of righteousness."** God's lovingkindness is better than life itself, invoking praise from our lips (Ps 63:3). In Psalm 88:11, the lovingkindness of God is argued against God's judgment. The judgment here is death and the grave. The mercies of the Lord are a song in the heart and the mouth of His people, and his faithfulness is known to all generations (Ps 89:1). Over 300 times in the Bible the love of God is extolled, His mercy over 200 times, His forgiveness over 80 times and His tenderness more than 25 times along with numerous other recognitions of His goodness. As witnessed by these Bible passages, God is very much interested in having man view Him in that way. Like the Great Person that He is, with great emotions, a great heart, the ultimate sense of fairness and justice and the exemplification — indeed the personal embodiment — of love in the righteous sense, God cares a great deal how all of mankind, and particularly His children, feel about Him.

God's Perception of Himself

The Holy Ghost has guided the inspired pens to tell us many things about how God sees Himself. It hardly needs to be said that this is God's instruction to us about Himself. It gives us special insights into the character of God and the importance that He places on his reputation in the eyes of men. We could be as tedious as we wanted to in bringing this to light through the scriptures, but perhaps a few citations will establish the thought. In Jeremiah 10:23-24, the Lord says through the prophet: **"Thus saith the**

Lord, Let not the wise man glory in his wisdom, neither let the mighty man glory in his might, let not the rich man glory in his riches: but let him that glorieth glory in this, that he knoweth me that I am the Lord which exercise lovingkindness judgment, and righteousness, in the earth: for in these things I delight, saith the Lord." Then in chapter 31, verse 3, God says, **"Yea, I have loved thee with an everlasting love: therefore with lovingkindness have I drawn thee."**

God's Perception of Man

Not only does God care about how man feels about Him, but God cares more than we can put into words about us. He wants us to know that He does what He does not only out of justice and righteousness, but also out of love, compassion and an omniscient interest in what is best for man in His own image. He desires greatly to have us know that His wrath and His judgment are the products of His love. In Psalm 103:13, it is written: **"Like as a Father pitieth his children, so the Lord pitieth them that fear**

Him. For he knoweth our frame; he remembereth that we are but dust." In Psalm 107, the Lord's mercies toward us endure forever. They are new every morning In Psalm 91:14-16: **"Because he hath set his love upon me, therefore will I deliver him: I will set him on high, because he hath known my name. He shall call upon me, and I will answer him: I will be with him in trouble; I will deliver him and honour him. With long life will I satisfy him, and shew him my salvation."** When we were yet sinners, Christ came to die for us, so that we, through faith in Him might be saved. This was when we were lost and undone. We were not looking for Him, He was looking for us. We did not love Him, He first loved us. Jesus loved the rich young ruler, even though he was an unbeliever who went away into the spiritual darkness.

God is very much concerned that we love Him and revere Him, that we know He considers Himself to be a loving, tender, patient, forgiving, caring God, and that we know of His great acts of love, generosity and deliverance on our behalf.

God's Wrath

But one of the very reasons for God's forgiveness, pity and patience, is His wrath. There are nearly as many scriptures in the Bible where God complains against His people for their inconsideration and evils and warns of impending judgment. A picture that omits His attribute of wrath, is not presenting the God of the Bible.

The Unity of God's Wrath and His Love

The serpent in the Garden was able to convince the human race that freedom and life are to be free from rulership, laws, consequences, duty and obedience to anyone. The Enlightenment concept of freedom is autonomy. We of the orthodox faith have tried to convince men that freedom in the biblical and ultimate sense has nothing whatever to do with autonomy. It has everything (and only) to do with God the King, Immortal, Eternal and Only Wise. Freedom is to be completely conformed to the laws and the kingship of Him who is Jehovah, The Life and the

Giver of Life, He who is The Way, The Truth and the Life. We have tried to point out to them that the humanism that was unleashed upon the religious world by the Enlightenment is utterly wrong. Reason is not the test of truth or orthodoxy. The Bible is the test of both truth and orthodoxy. Therefore, the conclusion that there can be no correlation between the love and the wrath of God because it presents a rational contradiction is wrong. God is love and God is wrath, God is forgiving and God is judgmental. God will suffer long, but He will not teach us bad habits, or let His Kingdom become corrupt by allowing evil and not judging it. Yet in the process, we always try to leave men with the realization that the greatest attribute of God (and the greatest attribute of man according to I Corinthians 13), is charitable love. This approach to teaching man truth about God is not only a privilege, but a duty and a commission. *God so loved the world that He gave his only begotten Son. Go into all the world and preach this Gospel of the Love and forgiveness of God to every living* _creature_. And so we cannot ignore as unimportant the way God wants man to view Him, and the way man does in fact see God in this respect. We do not go to the unbiblical and unsanctified ends that some do. We do not ignore the teachings of judgment and condemnation in order to try to reason or coax man into loving God. But it is not a matter that we can leave out of the formula when considering how we present the message of condemnation and judgment to unredeemed man.

If the feelings that men have about the doctrine of being tortured forever in an endless torment are brought on by the unequivocal and unavoidable truth, there is nothing we can do about it. But since the issue of the immortality of man is not a biblical but an emotional one, it puts an unnecessary burden on the mind as men try to comprehend the unity of the wrath and the love of God. And this, since it is unnecessary in this instance, is counter productive to the mission of the Church.

What About Justice

Not long ago I was reading an article on this subject by a man whose name I will not mention here. He was attempting to shame the doctrine of eternal destruction by appealing to justice. "Is Hitler just going to get away with it?" he questioned. "I suppose," he said, "that he will just be put to death and be no more. And so he will have gotten away with all of these heinous crimes with no punishment."

I feel sure that this orthodox, fundamental, evangelical Christian leader was not able to stand back far enough to listen to himself and see what he was saying, or how his argument sounded. Pay no attention to the fact that Hitler could have repented just before the bombs fell on his shelter and thus could wind up in heaven alongside this man; but I wonder if any loving Christian, after he has had time to think about it, really wants to take this position. Do you think Hitler's crimes can only be avenged by his suffering forever. Not long ago, here in California, a man was executed in the gas chamber at San Quentin. Was this man being let off the hook? Was execution a way of letting him out of his judgment? Wasn't it God who said that whosoever sheds man's blood unjustly and with murderous intentions should have his blood shed by man? Should we have marched in front of San Quentin, opposing the execution because the man was getting away with it and requesting that the authorities torture this man instead for every moment of every day for the rest of his life, that they do to him as the Mexican drug traffickers did to Enrique Camerena — that they should revive him just before he died and give him something to keep him alive so that they could torture him some more? Is execution, the ultimate forfeiting of one's life for his crime, not a punishment? This kind of reasoning is repugnant to every decent person, Christian or not. Yet this is the very kind of thing we are saying about God, without a sound biblical basis for saying it. Out of common decency we will not say, or allow this to be said about ourselves, and we will not allow our children to watch this morbid kind of stuff on television. Yet we don't hesitate for a moment to say it about God. I wonder how He feels about that, given the fact that the theological case to be made for it is mostly sentiment, tradition and guesswork. If eternal torment is to continue to be taught, I would hope to see a much more comprehensive biblical exegesis in support of it in the future. As of the moment, I do not know how that could be done, and I doubt that it can be.

How Is The Gospel Message Effected?

Some men argue that the absence of the threat of eternal torment is robbing men of one of the greatest incentives to repent. Those who do not believe that the Bible teaches eternal torment deny the veracity of that claim, saying that it is enough to tell them that they are forfeiting their opportunity to life that is eternal in its quality and quantity and that offers all of those things that men wanted in this life and never could achieve.

A few months ago, I talked at length with one of the most honorable leaders of the fundamental, evangelical Church in America today, and one who has been in the vanguard of protecting the dogmas of the orthodox faith. In the course of our discussion (which was really about a book I have written recently) he noted that I had left a lot of room for Conditional Immortality. I acknowledged that I had, and asked him if he felt this was unorthodox. He told me that he did not feel that it was outside of orthodoxy, but neither did he feel that it was consistent with what evangelicals are telling people in their Gospel appeal. I thought his comment about that was interesting and instructive. He wasn't so much in a dilemma about which view was the right one, but he felt that we needed to resolve the matter. If what we are telling people is wrong, he said, then we need to stop telling them that, and start telling them the straight truth of the matter. People should know what the consequences are and what they are giving up if they do not accept Christ and the Gospel. I could not agree more. We should resist the temptation to try to terrify men into doing right. The truth about the consequences of a deed are the most effective. The throbbing fear that grips a child if we tell him that if he wets the bed, the boogie man will crawl in his window at night, carry him off into the dark and eat him, is not the way to handle the situation. We can discuss the subject of capital punishment with people. They may not agree, but it is a civilized dialogue. They understand how decent and compassionate people can feel that there are certain crimes for which a man must forfeit his right to go on living. And they know that the courts have not held humane execution to be cruel and unusual punishment. No one but the most narrow, self-centered and insecure of persons would accuse those who believe in capital punishment of being barbaric and uncivilized, unless, of course, barbaric words and ideas were used to support it. But how far do you think the conversation would get (if the other person thought you were serious) if you began to advocate flogging with bits of metal, stretching on the rack, burning out eyes with hot pokers, boiling in oil, pulling out fingernails or skinning the man alive until the man simply died of pain?

Yet even this is more civilized than eternal torment where the man in question *cannot die!*

A Question of Omnipotence

If it is held that there is such a place of Eternal Torment over which God has no control, that He had nothing to do with establishing, and that He did not Will to be so, then in this view, God is not omnipotent. We are back to the *Barthian dualism* concept of an uncreated, preexistent, chaotic evil that is non-real reality and non-existent existence. There is an ontological problem as well, not only with respect to man's *being,* but *God's* also. This doctrine should be proscribed by orthodoxy, in my view, from the Church and to the real sources of its origin: Eastern Mysticism, Platonism, Philonism and other humanistic religious philosophies from which its fragments have been gleaned. I find it nowhere delineated in the pages of the Bible. One simply cannot extricate his concepts of God and how he projects the image of God to those he evangelizes, from the doctrine of Eternal Torment.

Wholesome Fear and Morbid Fear

The fear of being condemned and destroyed is fear enough for any man who is inclined to act out of that motivation. The morbid threat of an unthinkable, hopeless torturous punishment forever and ever does not evoke the kind of response that God wants from man. Though Jesus did warn of the consequences of sin and judgment, He never tried to threaten, scare or beg men into the Kingdom of God. He simply told them, if you want to go back, go back. Let him that is unrighteous, be unrighteous. This does not undermine the Gospel appeal, it elevates it to the level of civility and puts it in a context where men can think seriously about it from the vantage point of the free will and choice that God created man with and that Adam exercised in the Garden when he made his fatal decision. It makes the gospel approach to unregenerate men a civilized, rather than a barbarous dialogue.

Conclusion

The teachings of the Bible would seem to be clear enough on the issues of _sin, death,_ *corruption and judgment* on the one hand and *righteousness, eternal life* and *immortality* on the other. The unrighteous, who are under condemnation, will suffer execution and eternal death in the day of judgment. The righteous will be acquitted through the righteousness of Christ and will go on to eternal life and bliss. But the apparent clarity of these issues not withstanding, this is an argument that will never be resolved on this earth to the satisfaction of everyone, though it is resolved in the eternal councils of God (Rev. 13:8). This is not a new or startling statement; the ancients have said it and men have been saying it ever since. It seems incongruous with the convictions and decisions of the Church through the centuries that this or any other council should do what others have not felt wise or necessary, and attempt to close off dialogue on a debate that is far from settled in the dogmas of Orthodoxy.

APPENDIX A

COUNCILS OF THE EARLY CHURCH

The Apostolic and ante-Nicene Period

There is no record of councils from 50 A.D. to 170 A.D. From that date, diocesan and provincial councils begin to appear, but they were mostly for the purpose of local disputes. One of the first councils of note met in Carthage in 252 A.D., about which little is known. A national Synod met in North Africa in 255-256 A.D. to take up the controversy of heretical baptism. Three councils were held in Antioch from 264 A.D. to 269 A.D. against Paul of Samosta.

In 306 A.D. there was a Synod at Elvira, which pronounced 81 Latin canons against numerous forms of pagan immorality in current practice and in favor of Christian morality and church discipline. The 36th canon was an anathema against religious pictures being hung on the walls in places of worship. Many Protestants, through the centuries, have appealed to this Synod as an authority to object to icons, images and relics.

The first council of Areles was held in the South of France in 314 A.D. to appeal the decision concerning Donatism in the Roman Council of 313 A.D. Augustine called it an ecumenical council, but most historians feel that it was confined to the West. At Arles, Donatus was excommunicated.

The Council of Ancyra was held in the same year, in that capital city of Galatia. It was called in an attempt to heal the wounds opened over the Diocletian argument, with modest success at best. While in convention, it took up the thorny question of what to do to Christians who had given in to heathen persecutions, but who later repented. Of particular note were those who had given up the scarce and precious Scriptures to be burned. Many of the same bishops convened a similar Synod at Neo-Cesarea in Cappadocia in 314 A.D. to try to enlarge upon some of these issues and settle them. The going was so contentious and difficult that it lasted intermittently until 324 A.D.; with only 15 additional canons resulting.

Ecumenical Councils

Ecumenical Councils proper of the ancient Church (that is, those which are uncontested as universal in scope) began with **Nicea in 325 A.D.** Its theme was the Arian heresy and the contest between Arius and the great Church Father Athanasius.

It was followed by the **Second Council** which is better known as the **Constantinople Council in 381 A.D.** The purpose of this council was to alter and enlarge upon an article dealing with the personality and divinity of the Holy Ghost. The Nicene Creed probably resulted from this council, though there is disagreement about it.

The Third Council was the Council of Ephesus in 431 A.D. It met to condemn the doctrine of Nestorius concerning the two discordant natures of Christ, which it did in fact do, but did not arrive at any clear statement of the biblical doctrine. Because of that, it is regarded as the lowest in honor and character of the first four councils.

The Fourth Council was the Council of Chalcedon, Bithynia in 451 A.D. This council took on the Nestorian and Eutychian heresies, firmly established the true biblical doctrine as to the person of Christ in opposition to them, and enacted somewhere between twenty-seven and thirty canons. This was by far the largest of the first four councils, though it is generally put in second rank to Nicea as to importance to the

Church. Yet all of the Monophysite groups of the Eastern Church repudiate it.

The Fifth Council was also known as the Second Constantinople Council, held in 553 A.D. This Council, called by the emperor Justinian and rejected for the most part by the West, was poorly attended and never considered to be of much importance. It is ignored entirely by some historians such as Walter Elwell and C. A. Blaising.[30] The purpose of this council was to renounce Monophysitism, which the Church at large did not want to do because it was not entirely certain what the Monophysites were trying to say in opposition to the Nestorian heresy. "The Three Letters," having to do with three papers by men who had tried to defend certain features of the Monophysite doctrine,

---

[30] C. A. Blaising, *Evangelical Dictionary of Theology,* edited by Walter A. Elwell, (Baker Book House, Grand Rapids, Michigan, 1984), *pp.* 268-9. Here Dr. Blaising discusses 381 under the heading, "Constantinople Council," but offers no discussion of Constantinople II, nor is the "Fifth Council" discussed elsewhere in the book. On pages 2745, under "Councils of the Church," J. H. Hall mentions I and III but omits II.

were denounced also. Origen, to the extent that his Subordination heresy touched on the separation between Christ's nature and the nature of the Father, was also denounced as heretic. There is no evidence of a historical nature that any other features of Origenistic heresy, such as Restorationism, were taken up, though they might have been.

The Sixth Council (Third Council of Constantinople) was held in 680 A.D. for the purpose of condemning Monothelitism and restoring the purity of the old catholic Christology.

The Seventh Council (Second Council of Nicea) was convened by the empress Irene in 787 A.D. It was another secular-leader-convened council (emperors usually convened synods, but either at the request of, or in agreement with the pope or the bishop of Constantinople) that was very limited in scope and of no real significance. Its sole purpose and accomplishment was to sanction the image-worship of the Catholic Church.

Disputed Ecumenical Councils

The Greeks considered the **Trullan Council** (Fourth Constantinople Council) of 692 A.D. to be the Eighth Council. It was so named because it convened in a saloon in the imperial palace of Constantinople apparently called the _Trullan_. Because it established no symbol of the Faith and did nothing original, realizing only certain features of the Fifth and Sixth Councils, history has rejected the title of the Eighth Council. The Latin Church seeks to elevate the Fourth Constantinople Council of 869 A.D. as the Eighth Ecumenical Council. Importance is claimed for this council by the Latin Church because it deposed the patriarch Photius (an aggressive leader of the Greek Church) in a bitter contest with the Latin Church. But this falls short of legitimacy inasmuch as the Greek Church, which convened the council, annulled it in later years when Photius was restored to honor. The first Latin ecumenical council of the medieval Church in 1123 A.D. is also discounted by historians on grounds concerning which I can find little information. I take it therefore that one may include it or exclude it as he pleases. What its agenda was and what it accomplished, if anything, I cannot say.

Later Councils

In the more than one thousand years between 787 A.D. and Vatican I in 1868 A.D., Rome adds seven (some say eight) Greek councils and at least twelve Latin general councils.[31] Yet Greek and Roman alike are forced to admit that these were regional councils that made no attempt at defining doctrine for the worldwide Church.

---

[31] In arriving at Vatican I as the Twentieth Council, Rome would appear to be omitting all seven or eight Greek councils from the formula.

The Destruction of the Wicked Never Anathematized

Thus it is seen that no leader or council of the Church, from the ante-Nicene Fathers, to Augustine, to the present, has ever charged that the destruction of the wicked is either a heresy or outside of orthodoxy. It may be admitted that Eternal Torment is and has been the majority view. But it is not the only view of orthodoxy, and no one may say otherwise with Church history as his witness.

Bibliography

Works Relied Upon

Augustine, Great Books of the Western
World, Vol. 18, Encyclopedia
Britannica, 1987.

Douglas, J. D.; *International Dictionary of the
Christian Church,* Zondervan, 1974.

Elwell, Walter; *Evangelical Dictionav of Theology,*
Baker Book House 1984.

*Random House Dictionary, Second Edition,
Unabridged,* Random House Publishers,
New York, 1987.

Schaff, Philip; *History of the Christian
Church,* Volume II. Ante-Nicene
Christianity. WM. B. Eerdmans
Publishing Co. 1989.

Schaff, Philip; *History of the Christian Church,* Volume III. Nicene and PostNicene Christianity. WM. B. Eerdmans Publishing Co. 1989.

Strong's Enchaustive Concordance of the Bible, Abingdon, Nashville, 1980.

The Holy Bible, King James Version, Oxford Edition, Oxford University Press, Ely House, London W. 1.

Webster's New TwentSeth Century Dictionary, unabridged, Second Edition. The World Publishing Company, 1971.

Works Consulted Briefly

Ante-Nicene Fathers, Vol. I—Apostolic Fathers, Justin Martyr, Iranaeus—T&T Clark/Eerdmans, 1989.

Ante-Nicene Fathers, Vol. II—Hermas, Tatian, Athenagoras, Theophilus, aement of Alexanderia—T&T Clark/Eerdmans, 1989.

Ante-Nicene Fathers, Vol. IV—Tertullian, Manucius Felix, Commodianus, Origen— T&T Clark/Eerdmans, 1989.

Ante-Nicene Fathers, Vol. VI—Gregory Thaumaturgas, Dionisius the Great, Julius Africanus, Arnobus, Methodius, Minor Writers—T&T Clark/Eerdmans, Edinburg, 1989.

Barth, Karl; *Church Dogmatics,* Vol. III, Part I.
The Doctrine of Creation, T&T Clark, Edinburg,
1980.

Barth, Karl, *Church Dogmatics,* Vol. III, Part 2.
The Doctrine of Creation, T&T Clark; Edinburg,
1980.

Barth, Karl; *Church Dogmatics,* Vol. III, Part 3.
The Doctrine of Creation, T&T Clark, Edinburg,
1980.

Berkouwer, Gerrit. C.; *7he Triumph of Grace in
the 7heology of Karl Barth,* WM. B. Eerdmans,
1956.

Dowley, Tim; *Eerdman's Handbook to the
History of Christianity,* WM. B. Eerdmans
Publishing Co., 1977.

Edersheim, Alfred; *The Life and Times of Jesus
the Messiah,* WM. B. Eerdmans, 1990 (on Philo
and Philonism).

Lindsell, Harold; *The New Paganism,* Harper & Row, 1987.

Richards, Lawrence O., *Expository Dictionary of Bible Words* (based on NIV and NASB), Regency Refernce Library, Zondervan Publishing House, 1985.

Schaeffer, Francis A.; *The God Who Is There,* InterVarsity Press, 1968.

Schaeffer, Francis A.; *He Is There and He Is Not Silent,* Tyndale, 1972.

Schaeffer, Francis A.; *How Should We Then Live,* Fleming H. Revell Company, Old Tappan, New Jersey, 1976.

Shelley, Bruce L., *Church History in Plain Language,* Word Books, 1982.

Vine, W. E.; *Expository Dictionary of New Testament Words,* Zondervan Publishing Hosue, First Zondervan Printing, 1981.

Warfield, Benjamin Breckenridge; *Calvin and Augustine,* The Presbyterian and Reformed Publishing Co., 1980.

Whiston, William; *Josephus,* Kregel Publications, 1978.

Made in the USA
Las Vegas, NV
05 February 2022